The Burger Boy

The Burger Boy

Poems by
William Lawrence Woods

Cherokee Publishing Company
Atlanta, Georgia
1999

Library of Congress Cataloging-in-Publication Data

Woods, William Lawrence, 1958-
    The Burger boy/William Lawrence Woods.–1st ed.
       p.   cm.
    Poems
    ISBN 0-87797-277-X (acid-free paper)
    I.Title.
    PS3573.064523B87   1998
    811'.54–dc21   98-27961
                                        CIP

Copyright © 1999 by William Lawrence Woods

This book is printed on acid free paper which conforms to the American National Standard Z39.48-1984 *Permanence of Paper for Printed Library Materials*. Paper that conforms to this standard's requirements for pH, alkaline reserve and freedom from ground-wood is anticipated to last several hundred years without significant deterioration under normal library use and storage conditions. ∞

Manufactured in the United States of America
First Edition
ISBN: 0-87797-277-X
02 01 00 99   10 9 8 7 6 5 4 3 2 1
Design and Photography by Robin Davis

 Cherokee Publishing Company
P.O. Box 1730, Marietta, GA 30061

Dedicated to my late parents
Dr. E. W. Woods and Jacqueline Woods

CONTENTS

The Sparrow   1

Forever   2

Once a Spinster   3

Billet-Doux   4

The Runner Stumbled   5

Chance   6

The Burger Boy   7

The Ballad of River Jordan   8

Lacy Jane   19

The Hateful Heart   21

Façade   26

Benêt   27

The Bloughton Dog Massacre   28

Season   31

The World Which Broken Awaits Them   32

On the Horizon   33

Sunshine   35

Goodbye   37

The Someone   38

Two Are Dead Instead of One   39

Save   41

The Lady Cries   43

A Galileo Thermometer   44

The Storm Has Passed   45

Kiki and Didi   46

A Fitting Rebuttal to W. B. Yeats   47

Sadie Came Home   49

The Time Ago   53

R.I.P   54

Cold Requiem   55

Gone But Not Forgotten   57

Lines   58

ACKNOWLEDGMENTS

The author would like to recognize the following individuals for their assistance in this collection: Bill Baxter, Harold Gooldin, Robin Davis, Nancy and Slavko Chakovan, Dr. Gary Schatz and Bebe Schatz, and the staff at the Islander's Gallery of Treasures, on Saint Simons Island, Georgia. Keep on smiling at the gallery. The staff at Metro Association of Classroom Educators. Jeff Cox. Phil and Betty Cook and finally, the late, great, Cliff *Flint River* Shanks.

INTRODUCTION

Poetry is life. The true poet is able to lay a scalpel to the soul and thereby create for the individual the raw emotions lurking beneath the surface. William Lawrence Woods, a fresh, new poet, has accomplished this task with clarity, vision, and insight in his first collection, *The Burger Boy.*

Woods first discovered his fascination with poetry as his muse as a young lad of sixteen when he penned his first poem, "On The Horizon," a work of universal understanding rare in foresight for one so young.

William Lawrence Woods was born in Atlanta, Georgia, in 1958 and was raised in Jonesboro, south of Atlanta. A 1980 graduate of Emory University, he earned his B.A. degree in political science and was a school teacher in Clayton County, Georgia for several years. Woods received a degree in law from Georgia State University in 1991 and is currently a member of the Georgia Bar. For several years he maintained a successful law practice in the Atlanta area. A man of diverse talents, he has recently focused on a literary career with a special emphasis on poetry.

The poet, an admirer of the Welsh poet, Dylan Thomas, has created a unique style of poetry stressing the classical ingredients of meter, imagery, and symbolism. He writes forcefully about contemporary issues in a universal manner. Woods is innovative, provocative, and unafraid in his treatment of sensitive issues facing our troubled society.

For example, the poem "Two Are Dead Instead of One" concerns the execution of Karla Faye Tucker in Texas in 1998 and serves as an introspective look at capital punishment, while "The Burger Boy," addresses the inner-city drug problem.

In "Once A Spinster" we have a clear view of the sad and lonely on the periphery of society. This poem was composed in 1978 while Woods vacationed with his family in the Cohutta mountains of north Georgia. He trained his poet's eye on a lonely woman in an adjacent chateau having a conversation with her puppet. Thus, she became the embodiment of southern gothic malaise.

In his study of literature at Emory University, Woods became an admirer of the modern poet William Carlos Williams. Woods borrows the use of step lines from Williams as a poetic device in "Lacey Jane" (1978), "The Sparrow" (1980), and most powerfully in "The Hateful Heart" (1998), and "The Bloughton Dog Massacre" (1986).

"The Bloughton Dog Massacre" reveals the poet's lighter side and playfulness in meter. The poem is rich in imagery and personification as we listen to the "giggling wind." This comical farce proves to be an enjoyable poetic experience for the reader.

For the romantic, there is the simple, yet elegant, "Lacey Jane." Woods employs the use of step lines to describe the passing of late summer into autumn as the "leaves are falling to the ground." The poem has special meaning as if one has discovered a pressed rose in an old book of love poems. In a more traditional style is "Benêt" (1985). Its centerpiece is a woman who is the classic case of the femme fatale who, though possessing flawless physical beauty, could not feel real emotions.

In "A Galileo Thermometer" Woods helps us admit, and come to terms with, the pain of relationships – the waxing and waning between friends, lovers, and parents in hopes of reconciling the conflicts within. Its imagery is profound.

"The Hateful Heart" provides an excellent centerpiece for the collection. Its energy is hard to equal both in structure and theme. The poem clearly outlines man's injustice to man. Again, with the use of step lines Woods creates the actual beating of a human heart as "it beats, and it beats." In it the reader experiences the tragic events of history: Selma, Kent State, My Lai, and the death camps during the Nazi regime. There is a scary, macabre feeling to the piece and we are left to wonder if the cycle of hate can ever be broken.

However, "The Ballad of River Jordan" will prove to be an opus for Woods. This epic southern tale about the fictitious preacher, River Jordan, takes the reader into a world rich in old southern religious folkways and symbolism. The poem accentuates the fertile imagination of the poet along with his skillful use of vocabulary to set a certain mood for the reader. Its length and structure point to maturity and discipline. The ballad is also replete with hidden theological treasures if one chooses to explore them.

The poem "Lines" may also win national acclaim for Woods as a powerful example of free verse describing the aging process. It is the type of poem that requires several readings.

For the sports lovers there is the poem "Season." The 1978 Georgia–Georgia Tech gridiron classic featuring Georgia's Scott Woerner and Georgia Tech's Eddie Lee Ivery is now a matter of sports history. It was the inspiration for "Season." Woods, an avid Georgia fan, was present on the Georgia sidelines during the game.

In "Sadie Came Home" the poet takes full aim at the subject of incest survival – a topic much heralded in the media today. Sadie, a fictional character, is attacked by her own father and left to "brave the Wisconsin snow." She represents the victimized children we have seen along the way.

William Lawrence Woods, a deeply spiritual and dedicated Christian, includes in this collection several poems that underscore his personal eschatology. "A Fitting Rebuttal to W. B. Yeats" is directed at Yeats's famous poem "The Second Coming," while the poem "Save" represents the poet's quest for a deeper spiritual statement.

"Kiki and Didi," evinces the poet's respect for his late parents to whom this collection is dedicated, and describes the inevitable cycle of life and their timeless love for one another.

In *The Burger Boy* William Lawrence Woods has given us the courage to explore new vistas of the soul as we celebrate the constants of life: joy, love, delight, pain, and fear. We look forward with a great deal of excitement to the release of his first novel, the comedy, *Backdoor*, due for release next year.

In the meantime, relish *The Burger Boy*.

Bill Baxter

The Burger Boy

THE SPARROW

There's a sparrow on the ledge,
A faltering, awkward fowl
Awaiting his greatest test,
Whether to fly or stay within the nest.
Before there were two that cheered him on,
    Then one,
        Then all were gone.
And determined to recall those
Better days of a braver, gallant bird
He moved closer to the edge,
Resigned to do his worst or do his best,
Not failing to remember
How when last he leapt he landed
    Belly up,
The sparrow strengthened his
Tentative grip,
    Then,

        Jumped.

FOREVER

Forever is a feathered angel
   Along the streets of gold,
A speeding eagle climbing higher
   As its wings unfold,
A burning star,
   The way two lovers embrace
Before a gentle rain,
   Forever is the word we use
Again and again.
Forever is a young man dreaming
   Before his dreams grow old,
A racing tide of silver moonlight
   As it dances upon the shore,
A baby's touch,
   The perfect innocence
Of a child who cannot sin.
   Forever is but a short time said,
Yet a word that has no end.
Before the fall,
   And after the final inclement weather,
That will be
   Forever.

ONCE A SPINSTER

Once set eyes on a spinster
Her face lined with loneliness,
Painted with the sinister
That had painted old Roundtop for years,
And with her a small friend made of wood,
Which scarce made sense to others,
For only she understood,
How she made conversation
With her splintered beau by the fading candlelight
Rocking slowly and patiently as though
Her man of flesh would somehow return.

For seven years she waited,
For seven years she rocked,
With her friend of wood
On the Roundtop so the story goes.
In her eyes were the fears
Of the coming years,
Then her waiting stopped.

BILLET-DOUX

A billet-doux
For the one who chose to love
Among the ruins of a former storm,
Who dared to bridge the raging waters
Of passion too soon gone,
Who stayed with endless devotion,
During the fury before the calm
For all this and what will be
A finely sculptured two,
A love story,
　　To be continued later,
For you,
　　And more to follow,
　　　A billet-doux.

THE RUNNER STUMBLED

There comes a time to take a step up,
    To break from the pack into an open field run,
To heed a distant calling which before has never been,
    The runner stumbled hard but stood up again.
His tumbled ego bled tribute to the steps
    Which he had lost,
In falling he tarnished the gleaming glitter
    That adorned his winning past,
No longer a portrait of grace or exceedingly fast,
    The runner stumbled hard but did not finish last.
And as he lay there in the unforgiving heat,
    Dazed and unrefined,
Second by second he fell further behind,
    Though once a swifter, forgotten paradigm
With the race still in his heart,
    His weary legs placing doubts upon his mind,
Leaving his old life for a new one
    The runner shook the dust from his loins,
Raised himself,

    Then sprinted on.

CHANCE

Chance,
A timeless date with the distant stars;
One last dance to soothe an aching heart
That time has failed to heal,
One last chance to feel,
To have the love, when in dreams,
Is lost before the dawn;
A chance before we die
To tell the world we lived,
To have the unrelenting vigor
That was our youth,
Make us young again,
One last chance to win,
To play with fire and not be burned,
To dive into deeper water
And leave a final breath,
Chance,
A mountain seldom climbed,
A rapid rarely braved.

THE BURGER BOY

Swept from his mind was a horrible ghost,
A fallen lad who in past had been tame,
Sent swiftly to hell by a ghastly host
Never to speak that nefarious name,
The Burger Boy across the pagan way,
A burger boy to the Lord a stranger,
Who had known him once but turned away,
A true salesman now for Satan's rangers,
Led the lad on to a torturous fate,
One too willing for him he knew to chose
Taken without minutes lost to death's gate
Yet did not join the cast of other fools
Sentenced to die young alone or to rot
Trapped by spirits of that evil rock.

THE BALLAD OF RIVER JORDAN

Big and burly were his shoulders.
From the smallest seed
Sprang the mightiest of oaks.
There was nothing which he
Could not do,
And if he did not do it,
Then it wasn't important.
He knew how deep the waters were,
His name was

     River Jordan.

The offshoot of the strongest cedar branch,
A Cedar of Lebanon, tall and grand,
From Great Granny Rich and Pappy Dan,
Racing down the tree through Big Wesley
And his wife, Mary Ann, came a mountain of a man,
Six-foot-nine and still growing,
Whose shadow would engulf the others.
In time the world would come to know him,
His name was

     River Jordan.

Struck by lightning and left to die,
Almost crippled and almost blind,
He cried out for almighty forgiveness
Then reached his hands up towards the sky.
He put on the armor of his Lord
And placed his riotous ways behind,
Out of the fish of Jonah he climbed
This extraordinary man,
And they called him

River Jordan.

Healing with the power of his hand
They hurried from near and far,
Through the cities and the hinterlands,
Around the world, from distant lands.
It was his nature to stomp out
The smallest of divinations,
His courage would change a nation.
He was the Devil's great misfortune,
They all came to take a glimpse of

River Jordan.

Ten thousand were saved in
One calling alone,
They walked, they talked,
They ran.
Never was there a greater man
To be touched by the miracles of God,
Who held hands with the Man of Bethlehem,
And threw boulders at the stars for fun,
His name was

    River Jordan.

Eating fried chicken with turnip greens
In overalls, quoting the Bible and Vernon Johns
From the palm of his hand,
There had never been a preacher called
That could match this man of Abraham.
He parted the sea when he breathed a breath,
Then strolled through its muddy trench
With a holy resignation,
Big Wesley and Mary Ann's son,

    River Jordan.

Without needless hesitation
Or useless recitation he shouted the Word
For the lost, beguiled, and transient sheep of God,
With his staff and his rod,
The unequivocal truth he demanded,
For apologetics was not his forte
Or steady stay of hand,
From the spring of truth, sprang this simple man
And his name was

    River Jordan.

Who sang perfect bass,
Though *Amazing Grace*,
Rock of Ages,
And *Go Down Moses*
Were the only hymns he would allow,
He sang hard and he sang loud
As he shook the sky and shook the ground.
Miles away they heard his reverberations,
This man's name was

    River Jordan.

Ever vigilant in his repudiation
Of the vices Satan held before him,
He abstained from profanity and its locution.
With his stainless constitution,
His words were stern but not rebuffed,
He was the diamond in the rough,
The one who made the demons run,
A man of monumental proportions
And they called him

River Jordan.

Receiving divine revelation
He cast his shining pearl before swine.
Without a tremor and without emotion
He changed hearts and he changed minds.
Their friendships he accepted,
Though acclamations he declined.
His mission was to spread the gospel,
Not curry for exaltation or devotion,
And his name was

River Jordan.

He shunned the inevitable assignations
From the lilies of his congregation,
Of their alluring scent
He had not the slightest inclination,
Solid as a rock he was
Despite their numerous invitations.
The unconditional discipline
Of his flock was more important,
His name was

    River Jordan.

Unlike the jack legs and their palaver,
They lacked his style and they lacked his power
To accuse the shirkers, the trucebreakers,
The false accusers, the incontinent and despisers of God
They were pulled from the back pew
To the front by his simple, loving nod.
With little fanfare or commotion,
They sat without a whisper
And they sat without motion, for

    River Jordan.

His waters of life were full and overflowing,
Teeming with grace like his Savior before him.
Down by the lake they lined the shores
To drink from his fountain and to be immersed,
He flamed their fire and he quenched their thirst.
Never were so many slain in the spirit,
Their bodies trembling with the palsy
Of eternal salvation newly won
With the help of

River Jordan.

Falling giddy with the gift of tongues
They sought his timely interpretation.
He stepped forward with determination
Then turned their bubbling water to wine.
A heavenly declaration spilled forth,
Well expounded and well defined,
An unpretentious oblation
For the Father and the Son,
With a lot guidance from

River Jordan.

With every knee bent
And every head bowed
His righteous tongue bellowed with hope.
It held the cure for their hangdog blues,
He could make the mountains hide
And he could make the oceans move.
With the resoluteness of his faith
He could have doused the burning sun,
No one doubted the elevation of

River Jordan.

Never failing in his sacred dedication
He wrestled with the haughty serpents
And forced their expiation.
They danced with fear, then danced with pride,
With the mark of his heavy lumber upon their scales,
He laid them low, then he raised them high.
Not a word was spoken about his methods,
He knew the how and he knew the why,
And his name was

River Jordan.

Always at battle for the one lamb gone astray
He competed with the forces of darkness
With his swifter, deadly verse,
They ran there hard, but he got there first,
Then stared them down with a steely indignation.
His confluence of tears would then confound them
As he welcomed his waiting prize back into the fold,
Never before or since his Father roamed
Had they seen the likes of

    River Jordan.

Avoiding the wicked perversions
Of the wizards with their godless diversion
He harried their evil numbers
Without mercy or absolution,
They were given no quarter
Where his saintly pulpit stood,
Where his fertile soil spread, they had no root.
He knew the dangers of their evocations,
And his name was

    River Jordan.

Through the constant veil of sin,
The travails of drunkenness, idleness,
And their many tragic friends,
Amid the raging storms of life
He was the calming wind.
The chosen would fall silent when he passed
And when he called them forth, they went.
They knew his work and they knew the man,
And they called him

River Jordan.

Upon his sweaty brow dripped
The toil of undaunted perseverance.
He knew when the milk wasn't clean,
Why the earth spun around
And why the grass was green.
He was the only one they would remember,
The fiery, burning ember,
The first, the last, the strong and sturdy timber
Known as

River Jordan.

Who flailed the fallen angels
Then sent their evil scurrying henceforth
Into the hopeless abyss of hell,
The Lord had been better to them
Than they had been to themselves
When he sent his mover and shaker
His vigilant proxy, the faithful one,
The highly reputable, indisputable champion
Known as

River Jordan.

The one for whom
The pearly gates would gladly open wide,
Then pause with silent reverence
As he finally stepped inside.
Heaven would grow impatient
For the pleasure of his immortal soul,
Alleluia, divine the glory! His work was never done.
He knew how deep the waters were
And his name was

River Jordan.

LACY JANE

It's autumn dear,
And the leaves will soon

    Be

        Falling

           To

               The

                   Ground.

Tearfully I recall places
Now left behind.
With each passing day
Your memory becomes
More of a memory.
With each passing day
Your face slowly fades away.
The flowering fields
That we once trod

Have long since ceased to flower
And only your name remains,

Lacy Jane,

The leaves

Are

Falling

To

The

Ground.

Come back to me.

The Hateful Heart

With hardened lives they come,
With sharpened knives they march,
To the hideous three-time cadence
That is the hateful heart.

    Say the terror now among us,
    Is the horror that we send,
    Say the terror now among us,
    Is the child of our sins,
    For the men they seek to bind us,
    And the men they do succeed,
    For the men they seek to hang us,
    And force us to our knees.

        And it beats,
            And it beats,

On our restless lives it feeds,
Hear its steady wretched beating,
Its violent, bloody seething,
It cares not for the pain that it leaves,

For the enemy is always ready,
For the enemy is always near,
For the enemy will always find us,
If we allow him to proceed

>And it beats,
>>And it beats,

On the stains of Calvary it creeps,
It was present at Selma on that bloody bridge,
And on Kristall Nacht ran free,
Hear its wicked incantations,

Its plumping, thumping speed,

>Say the evil now among us,
>Is the evil from within,
>Say the evil now among us,
>Is the evil that he sends,

>And it beats,
>>And it beats,

It beats on our city streets,
It was alive and well at Kent State that day,
And reared its head at Watts again,
Hear it in its lonely cavity,
Feel the misery that it sends,
It breeds its fear with a reckless hate,

The endless agony it expends,

   As it beats,
    And beats,

Awake and feel its grief,
Arise and hear its screams,
At Oklahoma City,
It walked,
And talked,
And breathed,
All is laid waste before it as it continues

To shed the blood of millions,

      And it beats,
         And beats,
            And beats

On the innocent ones it always bleeds,

      At Auschwitz,
         At Dachau,
            And Ravensbrück

It beat its deadly beat,
It bled its wrath at Sand Creek and Malmedy,
At Beijing and My Lai,
Watch its list of horribles,
Its insidious parade of lies,
Through history its wicked valves have remained,
To murder and wreck and shame,
As it
      Beats,
         And beats,

For the men who seek to bind us,
Are the ones we seek to please,
The neighbor sneaks behind us,
To drive us to our knees

And it beats,
And it beats,

With hardened lives they come,
With sharpened knives they march,
To the hideous three-time cadence
That is the hateful heart,

And it beats.

FAÇADE

Ah, cherish the days
In early spring when
The roses bloom and men
Are yet giggling boys
Doused in perfume
By the maids of tickling love,

       So it was.

Before the wretch gazed
Into a mirror
To worship an image
She valued more than life
And her beloved,

       Wicked mirage.

BENÊT

Benêt could not be true
Despite her stainless beauty
Like a sword she drew
Around her silver halo there arose an ugly hue,
Benêt's bright lamp burned excessive fuel.
Her armor kept her courtiers few
For the virtue she wished most in others
Was one she never knew.
Every word was a poisoned arrow.
From her feigning tongue they flew.
Not a vow she kept, read her lover's tomb,
Benêt could not be true.

THE BLOUGHTON DOG MASSACRE

Something in the wind foretold its coming,
The ill midnight it served, trembling, said nothing.
Still it came that night
On the sun-drenched streets of Bloughton,
Oh what strange things may be,
When the giggling wind tickles the lonely tree
And the sun is for hours delayed.
It was the time of day when the hounds chose to stay
On the dusty downtown streets of Bloughton.

    Now everyone knows,
    That good dogs stay
    Away from the road,
    During the dog days.

Without a whimper or a cry
So peaceful did they lie,
Those little canines without a thought
For what was soon to be their hapless fate
When that wicked invention of Henry Ford
Came speeding down the way

Building, building it was to a more frantic pace,
Full throttle with the hammer down onto the main street
Of Bloughton without delay.

But everyone knows
That good dogs stay
Away from the roads
During the dog days.

A dog's life is really not so bad
Given the right brand of luck.
It could even be nice,
In the right time with proper care,
But not in Bloughton and not on that night,
When the dust masked the hot, scheming August air
In the heat of the dog days.
Without a whimper or a cry
So peaceful did the hounds lie,

But everyone knows
That good dogs stay
Away from the roads
During the dog days.

Nothing can resemble the sound
Of crunching canine whining,
The '57 Chevy grinding,
Over what lay directly before it.
The dogs in their deep slumber ignored it,
Just yawned and dreamed and snored through it,
Too late to move, too late to jump,
The memories of their shortened lives
Would not be enough,

Nothing to remind the world of their contribution
Of how they sniffed and barked and romped,
Nothing to distill the midnight horror,
Or to quell the giggling wind,
Only a thud, a plunk, a thump,
    And then,
        Just,
            Bump,
                Bump,
                    Bump,
   Just,
      Bump,
         Bump,

            Bump.

SEASON

The time one spends
Mowing waning lawns
As they wave goodbye, pal,
To the summertime eye
Quick to greet the
Fall leaves' smelly smog
And the hardy howls of
Hunker-down, hairy dog
On game Saturday,
Holy Saturday,
Is the finest time.

THE WORLD WHICH BROKEN AWAITS THEM

On a mound of clay rests the potter's nails.
Indifferent to the jackal's foul call
That the anointed ones will always fail,
He spins a work that surpasses them all.
The world, which is broken, is much like that,
Where one mighty pen can change a whole life,
The world, which is waiting broken, is a fact,
Calls the gifted to come and claim their right
The ones that would only trembling detest
A thought so painful as being stopped
In a life which speaks little to the rest
Gather their tools for battle and go up
To a broken world which is waiting to mend.
Children of God go forth with pride, Amen.

On the Horizon

The sun sets peacefully in the West,
Venus sparkles at its greatest angle,
All work has ceased and there is time for rest,
Time to review one's life.

God's eyes scan the stage where good
And evil have been the players,
The instruments of his desires.

Slowly, the light sinks beneath the trees,
Darkness engulfs the thoughts
Of a lifetime.
In this moment a warmness comforts
The righteous protagonist.

Shadows dart and haunt the soul
Once beguiled innocently
By the follies of youth.

The nebulous forms are soon justified
By a ripe harvest moon,
Bright with hope
Gleaming with the emanation of knowledge
Previously hidden from view.

A gasp pierces the night air, followed by
The peace that passes all understanding.
The old has faded, the new begins,
Far in the distance the dawn
Was breaking on the horizon.

SUNSHINE

Sunshine came to us
  In the prime of her life.
Sunshine came to us
  We know not how nor why.
In a fallen state where we waited,
  Unpronounced and ill-defined,
Sunshine was a shining star
  That led us through the night.
Her radiant beauty came unexpected,
  Her unbridled charm was unrehearsed.
Sunshine was a breath of hope
  In our dull and dreary world.
With the kindness of her nature
  She made us touch the sky
  And race the wind.
Sunshine came to us on a summer night
  To help us live again.
If only our words could have shown her
  What hearts could so describe,
They still would have fallen short
  Of what it really meant
When Sunshine stepped into our lives.

Our restless days seemed brighter then
    And when she smiled we all fell quite.
Sunshine came to us as a gift from God,
    We know not how but why.

GOODBYE

Goodbye, the most despised of words,
Is hard to say,
When those who are bound by
More than words
Must turn and walk away,
So we say until next time,
Though we know that next time never
Really comes.
For goodbye, despite its cleverly cloaked disguise,
Always means goodbye,
For those who have loved as we
There can be no end,
Yet we say it,
Goodbye,
In another time with another love
Would mean nothing
So perhaps we should not indulge it,
Perhaps it would be no more a lie
When parting next with one so dear
We said simply,
Gone,
    With no goodbyes.

THE SOMEONE

There is a someone,
A one we wish to hold,
The long-awaited someone
Lost among the fold,
Who seeks a distant calling
From another still unknown,
Another lonely someone
Within the same lost fold.
As yet we do not see them
Our hoping bids us to wait,
The other lonely someone
May be just beyond the way.

TWO ARE DEAD INSTEAD OF ONE

Fire the cannon, boys,
  Strike the drums,
Now two are dead
  Instead of one.
Despite the elocution
  From the hardened right and left,
There seemed but one solution,
  To make her walk the walk
Despite her resolution
  To love thy neighbor as thyself.
Deep in the heart of Texas
  That pickax bitch salvation won
Was led to her earthly death
  And finally left for home,
So wave your flags,
  Then aim your guns,
But two are dead
  Instead of one,
And the eyes of Texas were upon her,
  And the eyes of the nation were on Texas,
Then the slayer held his tongue.

For what the heart could have told
    That day if given a chance
Would have been in Austin
    Mere happenstance,
For whether right,
    Or whether wrong,
When all was said and done
    In spite of the dirges by candlelight,
Despite the sagacious song,
    Later when the night fell to the sun,
Two were dead
    Instead of one.

SAVE

Save was a good ol' man,
With the word in his pocket
And a hammer in his hand.
From the crib to the grave
He had a world to save.
From beginning to end
He did his Father's will,
And they beat him,
And they spat on him,
Then laid him on a cross,
While the nails he had known
So well in his youth
Were driven into him.
Only then was his work done,
Only then could it be said
That Save was not a man
But only half a man,
And half God,
Though only the elect
May understand

What the others will on that final day
When in the sky they view his raised hand,
For the world has waited,
And the world still waits,
Until, above the confusion and the clamor,
Down will come his hammer.

THE LADY CRIES

Beacon of freedom to the world,
Steadfast torch lighting the night,
Savior for the careworn souls
Your lady cries tonight.
The burden upon her proud shoulders
No longer may she bear,
Beneath her buckling tendons
Breaks a steady sea of tears.
What could make a giant bow?
Will the weighted moment
Send her wailing into the sea?
Gracious land with gracious people
Open your eyes that you might see,
Far out beyond the harbor lights
With your flame fading in the night,
Beacon of freedom to the world,
Steadfast torch,
Your lady cries tonight.

A GALILEO THERMOMETER

Waxing and waning, hot and cold, we were
Up and down with mercurial unrest
Like a Galileo Thermometer,
Its workings never at true peace or rest
The temperature rising high, then falling,
An unstable barometer of rage,
Then affection, boiling, then calming,
Inconsistent by moment and by day
The constant vexations of our proud blood
Mixed the bright colors intemperately
Exchanging quickly and misunderstood
With never a true measurement to read.
So much did I love her despite the pain,
So much did she love me despite the same.

THE STORM HAS PASSED

Open your eyes now
    The storm has passed,
The one that brought her to you
    Comes to take her back.
Wish not to know the answer,
    Hold fast young man, hold fast,
That same all-knowing force
    That brought her to you
Now comes to take her back.
    And yes, a man is strength,
But none shall come when at last,
    The one that brought her to you
Comes to take her back.

KIKI AND DIDI

Kiki and Didi were joined at the hip,
Strolling through the jungle roaring they met,
Beside the rolling water they soon crept,
There, the two knelt as one upon a cliff,
Then Kiki took Didi as her other self.
And together they sang the song of life
And together they shared its greatest gift,
A pride of young lions on that special cliff.

But those lions refused to lay with the lambs,
Sent roaming henceforth into harder times,
Then the world lost Didi, then Kiki as well,
Though in the jungle one could not have told
Because they sang their loving song, so well,
There roar is still heard through a younger lion.

A Fitting Rebuttal to W. B. Yeats

I cannot believe
He who has created shall not return
To reap the burden of his labor,
To ask of things we have done,
Of things we should have done,
But did not do,
To hold us in his embrace once again,
To care for us and wipe away the tears forever.
I cannot believe the wicked shall go unpunished,
That good and evil will sit together in eternity
As equal partners,
I cannot believe that God turns a deaf ear
To the anguishing cries of humanity
And that on the final day
His shout of victory will not exceed them all.
I cannot believe that a man had himself
Hanged on a cross to fulfill a vain philosophy
With his own blood.
I can neither explain nor justify this
To those who feel we are merely
A cluster of existential dust,
For the fool in his heart has said there is no God,

Yet I can believe that each of them,
From Sartre to Nietzsche,
Has called his name in their final breath,
And they called it with fear!
Maybe it's simple thinking,
But more than likely
It has something to do with that barn
Two-thousand years ago
When the love of God reached down,
And handed a little piece of himself
To mankind as a compromise.
Now that seems like a proper closing act,
And one that brings some sanity,
To all the madness.

SADIE CAME HOME

Why Sadie left home
Only a few would know
Sadie left us one chilly night
To brave the Wisconsin snow.
Sadie had been raped by a trusted soul
The why and wherefore only God would know,
So Sadie left home, that is all that was known.

Oh where oh where has Sadie gone,
Oh far away from home,
We love you blessed Sadie,
We love you please come home.

Sadie left home at ten years, no more,
A saint was Sadie since the time she was born
Brought early to the church awaiting at its door
So stolid and stunned were the elders whom she adored
When they heard of the horrible news as told
Sadie had been raped
And left in the snow.

Oh where oh where has Sadie gone,
Oh far and want go back,
We miss you blessed Sadie,
We miss you please come back.

No word was heard from Sadie
Her treasured countenance grew distant with the clock
Ten years and one had elapsed since that dreadful night
When the elders received a short letter,
Its contents too valuable to hide,
Naming the culprit on that night
And determined to uphold his lies.

Oh where oh where has Sadie gone,
Oh far away that night,
Oh father please don't do it,
Oh Sadie please don't cry.

How does a child live in a torn and sinful world,
Armed only with her innocence,
Shielded only with her curls?
Her strength was the answer to this riddle
Her hardened spirit and hardened soul,
Sadie had grown up quickly,
And quickly learned the world.

Where oh where is Sadie now,
Into the world alone they tell,
Oh where oh where is Sadie now,
Alive in living hell.

But Sadie was alive,
She wept until her tears ran dry,
She cried in the playtime of others
Though the chosen would not tell why,
Resigned now to a fate ordained from up above
Headed for her hometown on the outbound midnight train
Sadie defied the odds, shook her fist and still remained.

    Oh where oh where is Sadie,
    Oh far away from home,
    Oh where oh where is Sadie,
    Returning to her home,

Sadie was returning home
Moving closer through the night
The elders refused to tell the truth,
Or refused to tell it right,
How a little girl was left alone
To mend her fractured life, moving closer she was
With a purpose and a vengeance and almost in sight,

    Oh where oh where is Sadie now,
    Moving swiftly as on wings,
    Oh where oh where is Sadie now,
    Coming for the reckoning.

So it was years hence they told the story
Of the Wisconsin snow and her struggle for life,
How upon returning to her place of birth she placed
A knife into the offender's side,
The elders more convinced now than ever,
Not to tell the ugly truth or tell it right,
Some things were better left untold,
To protect an innocent life,
So it happened as she came striding into full sight,
When just before the dawn her resilience at last bestowed
Standing tall and proud and undaunted like her soul,
Sadie that precious angel, the little girl,
Who we had loved and known,

    Came home.

THE TIME AGO

Ageless and timeless
    Were the years spent watching
The cities grow
    When the stride hit the stride
In the time ago.
There before our clocks struck twenty,
    In a world we had yet to know,
Two hearts held hands together as one
    And never have let go,
        But,
            That was a time ago,
Before the world grew up
    And with it grew us,
        The time ago,
A crystal collection of the best
    We used to know,
And each of our secret recollections,
    From the first to last kiss,
        From the first to last sin,
            Are locked safely within.

R.I.P.

The day on which she had thrown away
    the love that I had sought
For her thunderstorm thoughts
    was the day that I had prayed
To pay the grave
    for my sins of gin,
Was the day when
    The Reaper leaped his leap
For the head of horns
    On the day becoming born.

COLD REQUIEM

Cold rain was falling,
I prayed to forget,
How the sky hinted of living death
With the news of your passing
On my weary heart
As fate dared to place us apart,
Now you to dwell without I,
In that perfect place
Leaving myself to the human race,

> Treasure the life without pain,
> Eternity does beget,
> For here it is raining,
> And the ground is wet.

Bold thunder was calling,
It made me regret,
The praises owed yet never said
Weak few gather ready
To mutter these belated words
Of how you lived your life
With sense and flair and grace,

While I stand with the others
In this melancholy place.

Frolic now, my lifelong friend,
Where light can never rest,
For here it is raining,
And the ground is wet.

GONE BUT NOT FORGOTTEN

Could it be
That life has ended
For one so good and true?
Here, a book was waiting to be read,
It was never opened.
A body that longed for tenderness,
Was never touched.
The mind and soul that so often
Refused to quit,
Finally did quit.
Could it be
That we are
All responsible?

LINES

Jets of blood, fresh and pristine,
Driven by the seeming immortality of youth,
Flow as an unhindered stream to fullness
Speeding through the veins
Without inhibition or hesitation
Keeping the surface smooth,
A perfect reproduction of Dorian Gray—
Before the portrait ages
And the pain befalls to exact the toll
That becomes the unforgiving lines.
Their course is charted before time began
Falling relentlessly upon the grieving soul
They come through passages
Of disconcerting memories
Their measurement is futile,
Subtle, like a silent, army of strength
Poised for battle, confident of victory
And so resigned,
Like the ticking of a slow watch
That has lost its enthusiasm
Moving less with each rotation
Knowing the force of gravity will overtake it
And render it useless,

Our flesh weakens and the lines creep forward,
Digging a crevice with each passing crisis,
A canyon forged with every unfortunate tragedy
Chiseled into the unblemished mountainside,
Unannounced, unwelcome,
Leaving a path of destruction,
Reigning havoc over the countenance
We held sacred in our salad days,
Unblessed, without glory any longer
We wear them but do not accept them
In their devastation rests the price of wisdom,
Upon our rugged landscape sits the cost
With honor they have been earned,
With knowledge they have been forged,
Taking us far beyond the mistakes of youth,
Yet it seems little consolation
Because damned and certain
The trenches grow deeper
Through the cruel passing of time
Random, but all connected
They run down the forehead, then past the eyes,
Tracing the jaw,
They feud and twist and wind

Like a thief exposed
We stand before the mirror without mercy
Awaiting the glorious graduation
unable to hide the lines.